BECOMING

WINE

GIVE YOURSELF TIME

By Que'Nona Guilford

Book Cover design by Bianca Brown
IAMBIANCABROWN.COM
INFO@BBVISUALBRANDING.COM

Editing by A.T. Destiny Awaits Group LLC
atdestinyawaitsgroup@gmail.com

BECOMING WINE

Dedication

This book is not just for women…As I decided to write this book, I was reminded of a prophecy that I was giving in 2012. I was in the middle of my mess when this man told me that women were waiting on you. I thought he was crazy, but the more he said it, I felt it. God has reminded me of this serval times. This was the moment I moved and started writing.

I dedicate this book to the waiting women that have been waiting on me not to be selfish but to surrender to my purpose. To the women that encouraged me until I saw God's hand on my life. To the ones that received the words that were coming out of my mouth and didn't reject them. The ones that covered me until I was able to stand on my own and didn't allow me to make a mess of my life. The ones that challenged me to be better and live better. The ones that cried and laughed with me, Prayed and fussed with me. The ones that pulled me and wouldn't listen when I wanted to quit. The ones that exposed my baby when I didn't know I had one. God has allowed me to go through a process to help you develop to your potential. Let 's go and be great!

Acknowledgments

First, I want to acknowledge and honor the God that has given me the ability to grow through grace.

Then my husband, Eureal Guilford, for covering me with his love and patience, teaching me how to slow down and endure every moment of life — loving all my broken pieces until I allowed God to make them whole. I love you with all my heart.

To my kids, Billie, Aaliyah, Noah (Naudia), and Joshua, I love and appreciate you. You all are the best part of me, and it is an honor to be called your mother.

To my parents, Howard and Anna Valentine, thank you for showing me the way and helping me be a better person. I love y'all to the moon and appreciate everything that you both have sacrificed for me. Thank you for showing that God is real.

To my spiritual father, Dr. Jevon Goode, thank you for guiding me through hard times and showing me how to move out of God's way. Thank you for believing in me when I didn't see myself and developing into a better woman, wife, mother, and business owner. I love you.

To my church family, Destiny Church Dothan, I appreciate you for setting a safe place to help me get delivered and set free from Satan's traps. Thank you for loving on me and helping me be better.

To my Editor, Tyeshia Thomas, thank you for allowing God to use you. A.T. Destiny Awaits Group LLC is necessary, and I pray it continues to expand into God's purpose. Thank you for your team's wisdom and knowledge to help shift your clients into bestsellers.

BECOMING WINE

CONTENTS

Introduction

G od will prepare you for the process before you even begin. I didn't realize how long this process was for me until I looked back at the dates and times; I went back and forth for months. You must be careful about slow obedience because God has a way of moving your feet to the place, he calls you to go. It is something about your wants and God's desire for your life. I have learned the hard way that God will override your thoughts. He never plans to hurt us because he loves us (John 3:16). His desire is for our better.

Processes are designed to pull goodness and blessings out of us. Through the process, you learn who you are and what you carry. You can't wait for the battle to find out what weapon you got. Wow, God allows you to experience things to prepare for the battle. Goliath was not the first battle David faced. He was fighting bears and guiding sheep at his dad's house. He knew his strength and who he was. So many times, we want to use other people's weapons, and we lose because it wasn't designed for us. Stop looking at the process as punishment and see the blessing in the things that you know as your strength. You must know who you are and what you carry. Embrace moments because there are nuggets in your process. A nugget is a tool you will need later or shift your perspective to be better. You usually feel it in your soul, or as my friends and I say, "my baby is leaping." Listen to God and move with him because this is where your grace and favor are. Learn to be slow to speak because God maybe still working it out. If you don't understand the lessons, Trust God, and as my mother said, "If you don't need it, put it on the shelf until you do need it." You can't go wrong following God. He is leading you to your destiny. You were made to win, so embrace the process. You got this, and God desires this book to guide you through your process, so you don't have to do it alone.

I have fought for months about writing this book because I don't like wasting time and didn't understand the necessity of the assignment. Meaning I thought people wouldn't support it or need what I had to say. Clearly, I was wrong because this book has already blessed people and changed lives. After sharing it with some women I trust, I knew God was up to something amazing and bigger than me. Thank you for loving yourself enough to read what God poured into me.

The title comes from a sermon that my pastor preached one day about the first miracle of Jesus. He talked about how Jesus turned the water into wine. He related it to guiding me through my process and how we meet and have conversations about my moves in business and life. I don't understand everything he says, but I trust what he says. He makes statements that change my life. He said, "I went through stuff, so she won't go thought it." This blessed me because I heard his heart and understood his position in my life. It is a benefit to have a leader that God appointed you. They are equipped with everything that you need. God speaks to them as they talk to you.

The second thing that my pastor said is he must make sure when they pour me that, they pour wine. I understood my assignment at Destiny and to the Nations. I'm grateful for Dr. Jevon Goode guiding me and letting God reveal it to me. He has kept me from some major mistakes and shown me how to believe in myself. The world was attacking him, but he was covering me. I will always be grateful for every word that he has poured into my family and life. We don't always agree, but respect goes a long way in our relationship. Becoming Wine is my process for the process of development through my pastor and spiritual father. Put your seat belt on and take this ride with me on a journey to healing, deliverance, awareness, freedom, and the next level of your life. God is up to something.

This is a movement that will help people get out of their heads and walk into purpose. Each word will unlock purpose and passion in your heart. It is my prayer that God expose and reveal things that have been holding you up from your purpose. I pray that He blows your mind about what is hidden within yourself. May God reveal your gifts, strengths, weakness, habits, and mostly purpose. I believe God will show you how to break things off of you that don't line up with his plan for your life. He will open your eyes to the work that you need to do. He will show you who is for you and who is against you. He will protect your heart from an attack that is trying to affect God's will for your life. I pray He gives you back your boldness and voice to be free to be yourself. May He give you joy and love in your heart. I pray that He delivers you from yourself and gives you room to love others.

I declare, You will stop overthinking God's purpose for your life and the plan that He gave you. You will walk into the best season of your life. God will heal every part that you hurt. You will leap into purpose with the boldness of God.

Grab your workbook and get ready for your change. Remember, change is married to growth. Your next is starting now. Decide that you will finish strong. Let's Work!

What are you expecting in this process?

_____

_____

_____

_____

_____

_____

_____

How do you want your life to change?

_____

_____

_____

_____

_____

_____

_____

_____

Name three things that you are believing God to do through you and for you.

_____

_____

_____

_____

_____

_____

_____

_____

Power of Deciding

Do you go back and forth about what God is telling you to do? Do you overthink the process and feel unsure about the direction that God wants you to go? Have you waited hours and days trying to decide which direction you should go first? Have you been hit by a different attack and don't know how to get up? Do you have many ideas and businesses and don't know where to start?

If you can say yes to any of these, this book is designed to pull you out of water and turn you into wine. It is power in the process, and it started with you deciding to be open to receive what God has for you. Let this book help and free you from the attacks that throw you off and slow you down from your purpose.

I used to be the person that would go back and forth and wanted to be sure that I was doing the right project. I started evaluating this process in my life. I realize it slowed me down every time that I was going to make a major move with God. I also understood that the devil knew me enough that this would slow me down when I made decisions to do something, it was a done deal. Nobody could change my mind and the more I seen my dream turning into reality, the more I wanted to move with God.

The devil think that he is slick. He started talking to me about me. At first it was small things with a low voice. The more I listened, the louder he became. I had to learn to start speaking back at him through God's word and Affirmations. I also use this technique with my clients because it worked in my own life.

When the devil is speaking you must speak louder. It is power in your voice, so use it. You must decide that the devil is not going to win. You must decide that he doesn't have the right to steal your joy. Anything that he does to a child of God has to have permission. Don't let the devil make you feel like he can do anything. Some things bring out boldness and power. Does God allow it, so we can be pushed to a better place? What have you allowed the devil to much territory in? Decide that you have had enough, and you want to walk closer to your purpose. Decide that you are worth the risk.

Book of Ruth in the bible is one my favorite books because it is evidence that God can turn your situation around through your decisions. Naomi lost her husband and then her two sons. Naomi was headed to Bethlehem, and she had decided that she was going release her two daughter-n-laws, Ruth and Orpah, to go back home to be with their family because she felt she didn't have anything to offer them. They both had to make a decision that day. At times like those we can follow our gut or heart. You can't allow your heart to lead you back to comfort zone. Ruth and Orpah had a decision to make. They could line up with Naomi's will or go with her. Orpah kissed her and went back home. That was the end of her story. Something rose in Ruth, and she said no "your people are my people" (see Ruth 1:16, MSG), and I'm riding with you.

God had another plan, and he was doing something through Ruth. Her decision set her up for greatness and stretch her faith. She didn't know what a head of her, but she decided to follow Naomi. So, she stayed true to the decision. She meets Boaz and her life changes because she trusted Naomi and her wisdom.

Let me bring this home for you because I believe in the power of testimonies and a personal story. This book is designed to be raw and relatable. I am a creator by nature and can do it in my sleep. Within a few years I have been blessed to develop a few businesses and have learned how to master multitasking. When God started dealing me about the world and nation Q's Touch was in its early stages, I was the coordinator, occupied with event planning and specializing in candy tables and themes. A Change In Me Inc Awareness Event was birthed out of my past experiences with domestic violence. Mrs. Que is designed to challenge people's perspectives and help them walk into their purpose. It also includes masterclass, my mentorship and coaching. It is the business that I have authored five books: The Moments When God Touched, Gleaning To Legacy: The Next Generation, Gleaning To Legacy: The Next Level, Leaping Into Purpose, S.O.S 30-day Devotional, Trusting God: My child to their Sailor, and Born 4 This. I am also a Mary Kay consultant that I use for ministry to empower women in business. Yes, it is a lot, and I love it all, but I want more and a deeper move.

I knew something had to change because I was making little money, not the money I desired. I had to step back and think about the bigger picture. God sent one of my best sisters to confirm what he was trying to tell me. FeLishia told me to focus on one. It took me a while to understand, but things changed for me when I got in line with what she said. All of the businesses are a part of me, and I didn't stop them, just paused them for a season so one could grow strong enough to hold the others.

Allow yourself to focus on one area to grow and bloom. Your future is worth it! Deciding is one of the most important things that you will do. It can make you or break you. It can turn you into the president/King or put you in prison. It is power in making decisions. It will shift your business. You must think beyond the moment that you are in and believe God has more. You must give yourself time to grow and develop when you use your energy for one thing.

Let me just put this right here. If you want to grow, change must come. I have not found one person that has been comfortable and growing at the same time. One day, I was driving, and somebody expressed to me how they didn't like how the city had just redone the traffic light. I amended that it was abnormal for our small town, but I thought deeper to myself and remembered when I traveled to other cities and never complained about a traffic light. Then I remembered my sister talking about how my mother would ride on a dirt road in the same area, and they had no lights. I just smiled and thought about when I previously worked at the hospital that was in front of the light. Back then, I was in my 20's, and our town was a lot slower and was just getting on its feet. I concluded that they had to do something and were preparing for the future of the town. And the person that I was riding with must be stuck in the past because people don't like change and don't embrace it well. I hated change and fought it every time I was near it, so I understood it fully.

Don't let your comfort zone to limit your destiny. You are worth the change that God is calling you to be.

What do you need to change to get there?

_____

_____

_____

_____

_____

_____

_____

_____

_____

_____

What do you need to decide today?

_____

_____

_____

_____

_____

_____

_____

_____

What Gift/Part of your purpose in this season is calling you to rise?

_____

_____

_____

_____

_____

_____

_____

_____

What change are you looking for in your life?

_____

_____

_____

_____

_____

_____

_____

_____

_____

_____

_____

_____

_____

_____

_____

_____

_____

_____

Delays will Come

Now that you have decided to move into purpose, you must be aware of delays. Delays can make you second guess your purpose. It will make you feel crazy and lost. On Sunday, my pastor spoke about being delayed but not detoured. He poured out so many great nuggets. I decided, with his permission, to share in this book.

Every person has a destiny. Destiny is not where you have been but where you are going. It is a forward movement into an ordained plan. It is God setting you on a path he thought about before you were on earth. It is the reason he has put you on earth. There are three things that every person with destiny will encounter: purpose, problem, and provision. Purpose comes first. Problems are in the middle, and provision comes last.

Purpose speaks from within you. Many people are afraid to do it because it doesn't line up with their pleasure. You must let go of things you have pleasure in.

Problems – happen to everybody. God is faithful to work through your problems. Don't be afraid of problems; all problems can be worked through. Just because you serve God doesn't mean you have a problem.

Provision- God will provide. Most of us don't talk out our vision; we talk out of our problem. It is in our view. When your view is obstructed, you must wait on the voice of the Lord. The voice of the Lord that brings clarity, decision, and power. Everything in your life is not destined. The Devil wants you to think that prophecy and promise over your life are going to happen in destiny. Everything is not wrapped up in a process. Some things are supposed to happen right the now, but you are going through a delay. From the Jordan river to the promised land, should not have taken 40 years. It was a 2-week journey.

If you are doing it by yourself, it can be hard. With God, it is easy to walk through it. Faith works; everything can't be delayed. You must speak victory over your life. Delay is not of God; it is the spirit of the devil. God has not changed his mind. It makes you fight for everything, and it takes you longer. You started accepting a level of life. You didn't' quit, you just accepted what happened. Things you prayed for, things you spoke over your life, and things that have been spoken over your life should not be delayed. God, don't use delays to teach you lessons, because it brings disappointment. When God is keeping you from doing something, he uses peace ahead of time.

Delays are aggravating and agitating. They will cause you to make decisions that are not for your life. Delays make you question the call on your life. Daniel 10:10, God releases the answer the first day, but there is interference. It is not God doing this to you. It has been some delays in your world. The devil doesn't want to change what you have in you. God has placed power and authority in you, and you have delays because the devil doesn't want it to come out of you. You must break through the delay. Deal with the delay and stay the course. You will get to your destiny. Daniel never stopped praying. The greatest thing you can do when being delayed is not taking the detour. God is not holding your stuff up. Keep praying and believing what God said, and watch out for the pits. Be who God created you to be, and you will have everything that you need. Some things can't wait. We must start speaking what God shows us.

What is your promise?

_____

_____

_____

_____

_____

_____

_____

_____

What did God say to you through the prophecy or confirm?

_____

_____

———————————————————————
———————————————————————
———————————————————————
———————————————————————
———————————————————————
———————————————————————
———————————————————————

I believe God for your life. It is Bigger than you. Keep speaking it and see what God says. The devil sends the delay to slow you down or make you give up. Don't do it! Keep moving toward your promise. God has not changed His mind. Satan don't win unless you give up. He does NOT have power over your life.

Will you allow the delay to stop you?

———————————

What is the delay revealing?

———————————

Is the delay protecting?

———————————

What did you learn in the delay?

_____

_____

_____

_____

_____

_____

_____

_____

_____

_____

_____

_____

_____

_____

_____

_____

_____

Position Your Mind

Have you ever felt like something was calling you? You didn't know what it was. In fact, you have tried to ignore it or Dumb down the moment. Well, you are not alone. You are not crazy, and it is something greater calling you. It is called your purpose, and I'm here to help you.

This part of the book will help you get out of your head, stop overthinking, and move quicker than I did. I have realized that I'm called to help the stuck, overthinker, and lost to walk into purpose. Be encouraged. Continue to stay open so you can transform into the wine that God designed you to be.

God uses moments to move us out of our comfort zone because he knows our flesh is a magnet to comfort. In comfort, we do not grow because we are not open to hearing or moving anything. For instance, think about a comfortable baby; they are not crying or asking for anything and are good. It is not until they get hungry that they start fussing and crying. It is a symbol that the parent recognizes that something is wrong with the baby. Now, the parent knows that the baby must eat or will get hungry within two hours or so. Some parents even have their babies on a schedule, and they are ready for the baby to get hungry. It has always amazed me that a mother knows what a baby needs depending on their cry. The parent never just feeds the baby because they need something to do. God is the same way. He is not going to focus on your life without an invitation from you. Jer. 29:11 says that God knows the plans for our life, but he isn't just going to knock down your door to tell it to you. What glory will he get from making you do what you need to do?

As a mother, some of my best moments were when my kids were obedient without getting upset. What am I saying? God is waiting on you to get in a place with him and seek his will for your life. Let your flesh die so you can walk into the greatest part of your life. Surrender to his will and find yourself in a place that you dream about. I know that it can be a scary and not easy process. The great thing is that you are not doing it alone. God is waiting for us to ask him about his plan and his design for our life. We must come to him like a child willing to be served spiritual food. God meets us right where we are and knows us better than we know ourselves. It is a difference between complaining and giving God the concerns of our hearts.

Think about the last time somebody asked you for something. How was their heart when they addressed you with their concern? Were they speaking through their heart or out of control and saying anything? Were they looking for an answer or just telling people's business? Were they wanting a change or just being nosey?

You must know the difference, so you know how to address a person. Don't let people just drop things on you because you are not a trash can. You can't think you know everything because if you did, you would be there already. If God has you on this earth, then there is more for you to learn. You don't want to spend all your days with less than what God called you to. Open your heart and allow God to fill you up. Get out of your feelings and let God fill you. What have your feelings done for you anyway but make you emotional and more confused? When I learned to check my emotions, my life changed, and satan couldn't control me so easily. We talk about checking our emotions later because that is a whole session. The more room you give God, the more you will grow closer to him. God wants to do so much for us, but we are too busy overthinking and being selfish. We are overthinking about something that he already has mapped out and willing to tell you. We are being selfish because we think we are on this earth for ourselves and not God.

What needs to change in your mind to get to the place that is going to produce your next?

_____

_____

_____

_____

_____

_____

_____

Are you ready for God to meet you so he can show you his plan for your life?

_____

What has God been revealing to you?

_____

_____

_____

_____

_____

_____

_____

_____

_____

_____

_____

_____

_____

_____

_____

_____

_____

Check Your Emotional State

Emotional- (of a person) having feelings that are
easily excited and openly displayed.

My emotions used to have me all over the
place, and I was so easy to get upset and go
off. The wind could blow the wrong way,
and I would shut down or fire up (not in a good way).
Listen, I'm going to be real and raw through here.
Have you ever thought you were going round and
round in a circle, then wondered how you were going
to stop it? When you elevated the situation, you were
the problem. YOU saved and still broken. If the shoe
fits, wear it until you outgrow it. One of the things I
had to check was my feeling and emotions. Your
feeling has you believing that people hate you and
they are not even thinking about you. You are in a
world war battle with yourself. Setting off bombs and
the person that you need to heal is the inner you.
Your feelings will mess up the best relationship or
slow down your process toward purpose.

I remember when I was praying to God about
my marriage. I used to say, "God change my
husband's thoughts and mind. He needs to do better
and appreciate me." I guess I was so perfect but
didn't have a clue. I was broken, lost, and had no idea
what marriage was supposed to be. I had fallen in
love with the image of it and believed in the princess
theory. (This is for a whole other book, but it is a few
people with whom I want to have a private

conversation). Why do we act like all a woman is supposed to do is marry, cook, clean, and raise children? Clearly, there is more to me and my life. I went from being mad and judgmental to surrendering and believing God. He refocuses my heart and my mind from being on me and shows me my faults and the path of healing. You have no control over the other person, but you can control how you respond or give your energy to a situation. It wasn't an easy process. Still, I am grateful that I decided to walk down that path. I didn't always pass the test, but day by day, I got better, recognized the traps of the enemy, and became aware of God's plan for our life. The devil has studied you enough to know what triggers you are being emotional about.

When we are emotional or in our feelings, we make bad decisions and prolong our journey. If the devil can't stop us, he will try to delay the process a few times in hopes that we will walk away. In relationships, he wants you to think one thing and the other person to think another thing. At this point, there are no moves being made, and you both are blaming each other. At the same time, the devil is somewhere laughing. He loves to use women's emotions and men's pride to develop a problem. We must be aware of the ticks of satan.

I'm called to challenge your perspective on relationships because it opens your heart to see the devil for who he is. Take your relationship out of his hand and understand your power. You are worth the work.

What causes you to get upset?

_____

_____

_____

_____

_____

_____

_____

_____

How long have you been like this?

_____

_____

_____

_____

_____

_____

Who have you hurt when you were emotional?

_____

_____

_____

_____

_____

_____

_____

If you had responded differently, what could have happened?

_____

_____

_____

_____

_____

_____

_____

What do you need to change for better results?

_____

_____

_____

_____

_____

_____

_____

_____

Who do you need to apologize to or forgive?

_____

_____

_____

_____

_____

_____

_____

_____

Be Bold, Prepared, and Leap

May you enter a place with God where your boldness rises. For me, it usually reveals itself through the storm because the storm provoked something in me. I never fully understood God's plan for my life, but it was revealed that there was more. I was that child that got popped for saying too much, not rude or disrespectful, just outspoken. The devil wanted to make me feel that my voice didn't matter, and it had me quiet for years. I have always had something to say. Being bold doesn't mean being rude or disrespectful. It is having confidence, wisdom, and being humble at the same time. You will have to sometimes fight against the waves and be confident that you are on an assignment given by God. At times, He will allow you to stay in the storm, so it will develop this part of you until you can control it. Later in this book, you will see that this is the lion side of you. Embrace this part of yourself so you can control it for your purpose. God created you to be different; you need to embrace this because it makes you authentic. Authentic is genuine, of undisputed origin. You are different on purpose, and God made you this way, so embrace who you are!

When I was in school, I never learned how to study. I have always regretted this because I could have gone farther with the tools. God has a way of teaching you the desires of your heart and making sure you don't miss anything. He has given me my desires to learn more than the basics of life. I find myself researching while I'm watching something on tv or something crosses my mind to do. You must be prepared this season in the field you are going towards. My purpose is to open my mouth and know that the information that comes out is correct. In order to do this, I must research what I'm talking about and extra. What if God wants to go deep with an audience? I need to know more. You must give God something to work with and a reason to use you. We must be willing to study our area and become more than average. Don't nobody need an average person to speak? I follow a gentleman by the name of E. Thomas because he has a drive out of the box. He is truly in his own lane because he chooses to be extra and has knowledge about pushing people.

When I watch his videos, it pushes me beyond my limits. Find somebody to follow in the field that you are becoming towards and study the way they move. God is unpredictable, so always be prepared. If you are not prepared today, then get prepared by tomorrow. Time waits on nobody. God can present you with an opportunity, so don't go empty hand. Make your moment count. Know your main things that matter and be able to explain your point of view. If you have a list of things to present, put your main things at the top because you may not have time to finish your list. Be true to yourself and be aware of your strength and weakness. This is your moment to make history.

Be ready to leap into purpose. Jumping into what God said you could have. Leap means spring a long way, to a great height, or with great force. God has been dealing with about leaping for a few years. I have written a book called "Leaping into Purpose." God has allowed me to challenge people's perspectives so they can leap in a specified direction. I'm challenging you to allow yourself to let your thoughts jump into what God plans for your life. Jump doesn't always mean movement in the natural. It could be movement in your spirit. Before anything is birth into natural, it must be birthed in the spirit. It started with you and allowed God to be God. Let go and stop being so controlling over your life.

I remember when God was first telling me that he wanted me to write a book. I really didn't think I could write because I failed English 101 in college twice, so I didn't think I was qualified to write a book. Our thoughts and plans are not always lining up with God. We must fire ourselves so we can be open to God's plan. I had to lose my thoughts and trust God's plan. I started walking once God gave me direction. You must wait on directions and when God wants you to move. I had to lean on his thoughts to write and believe that my story was necessary for another person. You must get out of your feelings and embrace God's plan. I look back on that moment and wow with God. Because now, I help other people tell their stories, and it's all because I believed God for the first step. I had to Jump in my faith to believe God wanted to use me. I had to leap past my belief and walk into my destiny. It has helped several people get the courage to write their stories. This process was one of the most powerful moments in my life. This moment was when my water started turning into wine. I started listening to my Pastor, Jevon Goode, and my thoughts started changing. God allowed me to go through the process so I could be better, not bitter. God started healing in areas where I wasn't aware I was wounded! Yes, he went that deep in my life. I would be on the floor every Sunday because my heart was hurting, and I didn't understand the process. I felt like God was punishing me, but I have learned that he was covering me. People would say certain things about me and didn't even know what they were talking about. I just kept going and getting the word because it was growing me to a better place. It was making me stronger and wiser. It was like God allowed them to throw dirt on me so I could blossom into a powerhouse. Don't worry about people just keep moving toward the promise.

People want to see the miracle but don't want to go through the process to receive it. Most miracles are from the press of the process. Be careful about what you are asking God for. Some things that God allows us to go through are to produce or prepare us for the miracle that we asked for previously. As you prepare your mind to leap into purpose, think about what it may take for it to come forward or what you might have to give up. Have a plan for what you are leaping towards. I'm not trying to scare you but to prepare you for the journey of unknown. We can be so excited and don't have a plan. Some of my best moves are when I try to think about the unknown. You can't fully prepare but being aware helps the process.

When you allow yourself to be bold, prepared, and leap into purpose, you start lining up with God's Will for your life. You will find opportunities and set atmospheres for miracles. You are the perfect package for God to send out into the world to share your testimony and free others from their life's limits. You will find yourself in places that you never thought you could go. Our lives are never without attacks or storms, but God rewards us with opportunities that are going to bless others.

What is stopping you from being in this place?

_____

_____

_____

_____

_____

_____

_____

Do you remember the last time you were bold? How did it make you feel?

_____

_____

_____

_____

_____

_____

_____

What did you like or dislike about it? Have you prepared for your purpose?

_____

_____

_____

_____

_____

_____

_____

_____

What will you need to do to Leap?

_____

_____

_____

_____

_____

_____

_____

_____

What is holding you down?

_____

_____

_____

_____

_____

_____

_____

_____

What lie do you have to let go of?

_____

_____

_____

_____

_____

_____

_____

_____

_____

_____

_____

_____

_____

_____

_____

_____

_____

_____

Destiny is Calling

God has a way of getting you out of your comfort zone so you can rely on him and be developed for his plan. As I look back on my process of transition, I'm aware of my belief and perspective that had to break off me. You can truly be in your own way. God could hold everybody back, and we still won't walk into destiny because of our mindset. I was so busy putting everybody before me that I left myself for dead. Have you ever felt that way? No worry if you ever felt this way. God will not allow you to die. This is one of the reasons I had to write this book. He wanted to breathe life back into you. It was nobody's fault but my own. I couldn't blame the devil. You must own your mistakes so you can heal properly and be prepared for what is next.

I had no idea some of the stuff God wanted to do in my life, and he was just getting started. I remember hearing this great preacher on the radio while I was getting dressed to go to church. Every time I heard him, something leaped in my belly. The more I heard him preach, the more I desired to meet him. I thought that he was from somewhere far off, and I wished I could meet him. I started trying to listen closely for his name but could never get it.

My husband told me that J. Bynum was coming to town, and I had always wanted to meet her. He asked if I wanted to go, and I was like, yes. I remember it like it was yesterday. The church had people everywhere. The church was beautiful, and its staff was friendly. My husband and I had to fit in a small place, but we were just happy to be in the room. If only I knew what I know now. I remember getting a glimpse of the pastor but don't remember anybody else.

I was at a place in my life where I wanted to know more about Bible. I ran across a Facebook page about a contest to get a scholarship to go to Destiny Bible College, and I overthought about applying for it. I decided to go ahead because I really had a desire to learn more. It was a God-ordained moment because I got the scholarship that changed my life. I was invited to the church where I would receive my certificate for Destiny Bible College. I remember being excited and didn't understand God was putting the pieces together. The radio voice, the church, and this certificate were designed for my purpose. God is amazing, and He loves his kids. I don't think that I was the only one getting a certificate, but I felt like I was. It was a moment in the service that I will never forget. God had already started dealing with me about the prophetic, which was different for me because I was raised in a traditional Church. One thing about God, he doesn't have any limits or borders. He is just God. The pastor of Destiny pauses for a few moments in the service, and I didn't know that was the start of something wonderful. God was up to something, and the world had no idea that God was moving. Then, he said that he would save that for another time. I remember God letting me know that it was about me. I guess my husband had his own moment because he fell in love with destiny and was ready to become a member. I was the complete opposite but excited about going to school and learning about God.

We were a house divided for a while, and it worked for us. I knew that was the church for my family, but I wasn't ready to transfer yet. I had some healing to do. I ran back to my father's church after an experience that cut me deep. I knew my father's love and that he had always done right by me. I trusted his leadership, and I was comfortable. I knew what they needed from me and what I was going to get from the church. I love the members and the church. God had another plan for the next period of my life. It probably took me about a year to transition.

I don't remember what exactly was caused this moment, but it happened so quickly. God kept dealing with me about Destiny Church, and I was still fighting the process. God began talking to me about the day I got the certificate and revealed that Pastor J had a word for me. I really felt that I was tripping in this season, so I just moved with God. He instructed me to ask Pastor Jevon did God tell him something about me while I was at his church. Now, I look back on this and laugh. When he inboxed back a "YES." WOW! It got real at that point, and I knew that I wasn't in my head no more. And things were about to be real. I didn't know much about him, but I knew that he listened to God and was obedient. It is amazing how God introduces me to his voice and anointing first. Second, made me aware of his presence. And lastly, he shows me his power.

It was about two or three Sunday mornings that my family was constantly going when my husband and I looked at each other ready to join. We had a period when we walked to church because we didn't have a car. We would be coming in late, and the church was so full that we would ask the usher to move us up front if they could. They started asking us if we would like to be up front before we sat down, and it was worth the walk. You never know what a person is carrying when they walk through the door of a church. We must be so careful when we are greeting new members. The devil doesn't want them to be rooted in the place that God has designed them to be. Most people, when they are in transition, are wounded and lost. They are trying to decide is this a safe place to heal. It is not easy to trust anyone when you have been through trauma. Just like domestic violence survivor has a trigger, they do as well.

A few weeks later, a Saturday, I had an experience that changed my life and broke any doubt that God wasn't real. I was on my way to a waterfall with a friend for some girl time. I love waterfalls and have always felt close to God through water. We had a breath taken experience in Marianna. It was our first time, and we enjoyed the trail and lake. We were on our way back when I felt a change in the atmosphere.

I asked my friend if she wanted to go to church with me. I just felt like it would be different, and she would enjoy it. When I got up that next morning, I bounced out of bed, and I don't bounce out of nothing. I woke up excited and ready to go to church. I looked in the mirror, saying, he is going speak to me today. Repeating, He is going to speak to me today. I still remember the title of the message, it was "I'm Determined," and that immediately spoke volumes to me. We sat at the back of the church that day, but we shouted our way to the front.

It has always been funny how I found myself in the front, no matter where I was in the church. We were so excited and embraced the words that came out of our Pastor's mouth. I had forgotten about what I had said in the mirror, but it didn't forget me. This moment hit me by some surprise and walked me into a different place. I had no idea about the words that were going to come out of his mouth. These words didn't just affect me but my whole family. He spoke to my past, present and future. They had me paralyzed and lost for words. Truly a moment where God revealed his love for my family. The more I learned about our journey that this prophecy would last us a lifetime. I had no idea his plan for my life, and he is still revealing pieces as I write.

God has a way of telling you something without telling you everything, and I love the mystery of God. On that day, I gained a level of respect for my Pastor. God can give you something, and you can't release it too quickly, so you must have control and wisdom. My pastor was already teaching me something.

What set place is calling you?

_____

_____

_____

_____

_____

_____

_____

_____

What do you need to let go of to get there?

_____

_____

_____

_____

_____

_____

_____

_____

_____

When was the last time a leader made your baby leap?

_____

_____

_____

_____

When was the last time you felt safe?

_____

_____

_____

_____

_____

_____

_____

Who is your spiritual Father, and Why?

_____

_____

_____

_____

_____

_____

_____

_____

_____

What do you have in command and not?

_____

_____

_____

_____

_____

_____

_____

_____

_____

What does this person pull out of you?

_____

_____

_____

_____

_____

_____

_____

_____

_____

_____

_____

_____

_____

_____

_____

_____

_____

_____

Live

The devil has a way of creeping up on you and taking the breath out of you. I had just gotten over Covid and was just trying to survive. It has been about a month, and I was pushing myself as always. I got hired to do one of my friend's surprise party at her house. On the way there, I just didn't feel my best, but I could not let my client/friend down. Once her husband entered their room, he loved everything so much that he wanted to buy the pop items too. I was so happy, but I was feeling worst.

By the time I got home, I couldn't breathe, and it got real for me. I remember telling my husband that I was going to ER. He knew something was wrong because I don't just go to the hospital. I told him to go to work and that I would be ok. By the time I got back to the hospital room, I was having trouble breathing and knew something was seriously wrong. I had texted my Pastor because I knew I needed somebody to pray for me. He told me that he would be lifting me and to play some healing scripture videos on YouTube. I did just that. I had started getting scared and doubting that God would heal me. During Covid, staff came in the room when they had to, and I felt alone for hours. By the time the doctor came in, I was ready to go. Well, she told me I wasn't going home for a few days because I needed to be watched closely. When she told me what was going on, I said that the devil was trying to take me out. I had one issue on top of another one. I was messed up for real.

When I got to the floor, it wasn't the same. Hours by myself, my family could not come see me. My pastor and family checked on me. I didn't have much energy and was trying to reserve it for the bathroom. Man, the first night was hard, but when my doctor came in, it appeared I was a different person. He looked at me and was amazed because I wasn't on oxygen and was looking like a regular person. He was looking at a miracle. He kept me an extra day just to watch me. I'm learning to live because tomorrow is not promised, and God said I could. Worrying never changes anything but the day that you die. Think about it. You will die a premature death by worrying. Not God's plan but your dedication.

God has a way of revealing Himself to you in an interesting way. You could be having a conversation, reading a story, watching a movie, looking into the sky, or just going a regular day. Then He appears out of nowhere. We will never understand His way or the reason that He does what He does, but He is so real to me. God comes to each person differently based on their needs. He is always ready to reveal Himself to you, but you must be open to hearing or feeling His presence. Our lives can change in a moment for the good or bad. I have learned to forgive myself and others quickly. Forgiveness is for you, *NOT* the other person. You free yourself from the trap of the enemy. When you don't forgive, you put a wall between you and God. It slows down your prayers being answered and your connection with God. It is like you started your journey walking away from him and don't even know it. Unforgiveness set in like cancer, slow but strong.

I went through a season where I didn't forgive myself. I thought I was punishing myself, but I was prolonging the time. When thing are revealed to us, we started looking at ourselves like why didn't we stop the people that hurt us? The simple answer is we didn't know what we know now. This answer doesn't help our souls. When trauma hits our soul, we must allow ourselves to go through a process. It is not going to happen overnight. Healing takes time and doesn't happen overnight. Allow yourself to breathe and reflect on the pain. Why did this happen? What can you learn from this? How can you prevent it from happening again? This is different from overthinking because we process things and apply the answers for the necessary shift of our thinking. When you overthink, you just think in circles and make no decisions or movements. You must learn the difference because satan will have you shooting down you're thinking. God has not created you to be ignorant so don't act or think you are. You are smart and intelligent, and God has more for you to learn and do in this life.

Some things come in your life to slow you down or throw you off, and you have decided to LIVE. Live in his will and favor with grace. Live in a way that makes the devil mad that your feet hit the ground. Live in a way that demonstrates to people around you to know there is a living God. Live to the point where people clearly know that the devil lied. Live to the point that your enemies are second guessing what they said about you, and they are telling others you are a blessing. JUST LIVE! You have been through too much not to live well. God said you can have, and your part is believing it is possible.

What experience the devil meant for bad, and God used it for good?

_____

_____

_____

_____

_____

_____

_____

_____

Who do you need to forgive and why?

_____

_____

_____

_____

_____

_____

_____

_____

_____

What is stopping you from living better?

_____

_____

_____

_____

_____

_____

_____

_____

_____

When did you stop believing?

_____

_____

_____

_____

_____

_____

_____

_____

_____

Who around you encourage you to let this belief go?

_____

_____

_____

_____

_____

_____

_____

_____

_____

_____

_____

Bigger than You

I got a call at work about a situation that brought my youngest daughter to tears, and really didn't know how to handle it. God gave me a strategy for us to start praying together about five specific things every night. I would start then she would pray. The very first time, she was nervous but did well. I understand now that this was getting her ready for the real world, and through this process, I understood the necessity of showing her that she is not under people's limits. God allowed me to see her strengths and guide her through her weakness. When she went into the military, I wasn't worried about her because I poured and gave her my everything.

The only way I can describe this process so most can understand is having more than one baby in your stomach because that is what really happened. My Pastor had prophesied on the subject several times and taught us so much faith that we all should have birthed something. I don't have a jealous bone in my body and was so excited and thrilled for other manifestations. It is so many times you can say…I'm next before you start wondering if you really are next or not. I remember this moment like it was yesterday. I want to help somebody and let you know that you are not alone. God had done many things for me. I probably would have stopped rushing it if I knew how huge these babies were. Frustration and irritation had pulled me into a place with God that would change my life. I never had a problem with thinking big. In fact, my husband used to get me to tell his friends about my dream because he thought, at the time, I had a big dream. It is one thing to believe God for yourself, but it is another battle to believe for your family. I was bold enough to have a conversation with God. I asked him one question. "God, do you want me to stay in my father's house? If so, please allow me to be content. Do you have something else for me? If so, show it to me."

Three days later, T. Moore came up to me with good news. Her parents had brought a house and needed to sell their house. She is an amazing person and will do anything for anybody. She went on to tell me that she told her mother that we would be great to buy their house. You know I was ready and willing to look at the house. I wasn't ready for the love that God gave us during this process.

Something shifts in me when my best friend/sister sends me a flyer of an opportunity to help us buy a house. She is not the type of person that you can tell her you are going do something and don't do it. She is younger than me but acts like she is my boss... I absolutely wouldn't change it for the world. She has made me better and helped walk me into my desires. She has seen me at my worst and still loves me, and that means a lot. She had brought a house about a year before, so she was the perfect one to push me out of the mud. A friend is not somebody that agrees with everything you say. A friend is somebody available when you need them and tells you the truth. If you can't be told the truth without getting mad... check yourself. She keeps me on my toes. She loves hard and gets misunderstood for it. It was several moments that I wanted to give up and give in, but Joyce wouldn't let me. She would reply, "So you are not going after what you want?"(She would ask this sarcastically). Then continue with "You ain't going to worry me." You can't do anything but laugh at her. She was in my wedding and fussed about that too. I believe besides my husband and I; she was one of the happiest about us getting a house. She just smiles like she was a proud mother...lol Get you some friends that you can cry, laugh, pray, believe, and grow with. She called and texted me throughout the whole process. She asked me did I turn in this or explained the things that I didn't know. She is the one that went with me to buy a Christmas tree for the new house that I hadn't put in an application to receive it. She just believed with me and for me.

Through this process, I doubted God several times, but he always used my Pastor's words and anointing to get me back in place. I never talked to my pastor about the heartache of some things, but he always knew what moment I was in. Therefore, it is so important to be under the right leader and know that God has connected you. One Tuesday night, I was frustrated and ready to throw in the towel because my husband and I were not agreeing on buying the house. Here a side note, everybody is not going to believe like you believe, and it is ok. Stay focused and watch God change their heart to what he told you. We think it is our job to change people, but God told us to believe. I had just had a moment with God before I got in the church and mentally just made it in the church. I just need more of Jesus. Tuesday service was amazing, and I was praising God for a word that my Pastor was speaking to an Elder in our church. He said "Furniture." And I praised some more. He said it about two more times and pointed at me. Man, my feet got light, and I ran and shouted until I hit the floor. ALL OF MY STORIES ARE TRUE. Then he spoke about me and my husband being on one accord and things were going to workout. Then I flew up like a plane and ran some more. God is faithful and will meet you right where you are because He doesn't expect us to be perfect, just wiling to trust him. By the way, my house is filling up with furniture just like my Pastor said.

I will not go into all the detail, but we walked into $30,000 of equity, Double sp ft,4-bedroom, 2.5 bathroom, Living Room, Family room, sunroom, Two storage, two-door garage, fireplace, three walk-in closets, and in our desired location. Only GOD! Our cat has even enjoyed this house better. He has his own entrance door on the back. It is a place that my children can visit, and we can make memories.

In the process, God unlocked my husband to express his dream and brought his job back. He restored my marriage. We have fell deep in love again and desire to build on this new life. God has answered my prayer and allowed me to be a better wife, mother, and person.

What is God telling you?

_____

_____

_____

_____

_____

_____

_____

_____

What are you scared to talk to God about?

He is ready to listen to what is on your mind.

_____

_____

_____

_____

_____

_____

_____

_____

_____

_____

What is troubling your heart?

_____

_____

_____

_____

_____

_____

_____

_____

_____

_____

_____

_____

_____

_____

What is calling for you to get in agreement with God about?

_____

_____

_____

_____

_____

_____

_____

_____

_____

_____

_____

_____

_____

_____

_____

_____

_____

_____

_____

You are Enough!

I have dreamed about being married since I can remember. When my husband got married for the first time, it was a simple event. It cost less than $600 for everything. My father is a Pastor, and he married us. My sister and I had on some sundress. My mother and I decorated the church, and it was beautiful. To be honest, the only thing I would have changed was my father walking down the aisle and wearing a wedding dress. I have dreamed and fantasized about wearing a wedding dress.

My husband promised me if I could wait until our 10th anniversary that we could do it all over. When we reached our 10th anniversary, I wasn't in the mood to renew our vows. I had become a wedding planner, and all I could see was the cost and labor of the event. My husband had tried to get me to start planning, but I just didn't feel it. My husband and I went out of town to celebrate our friends getting married. It was a breathtaking service, and it was time for the dad/daughter dance. It was a priceless moment that God used to minister to my heart. He began to reveal to me that the devil was trying to steal my moment. At that point in my life, I wanted to get everything that the devil had stolen, so it set a fire in me. I thought about the regret that I have about my biological mother, so I surrendered to having a renewal. We desire to be celebrated because we have overcome what most people divorce over.

I started planning one of the most important days of my life. I talked to my Pastor about helping us renew our vows. He was excited to help us because he had seen the hand of God on our marriage. When we first got to destiny, we were broken, and God had transformed us right before our eyes. He came out of retirement to marry us, so we were blessed to be loved. It was an honor to have his approval and willingness to help us. We honor our leader and respect the words that came out his mouth. This blessed me because I knew that my dream was coming to pass.

We went around Dothan looking for a place to have this special moment. We found the perfect place, but it didn't match our price. God asked me one day what I loved about this building. I quickly answered and said the floor windows. My husband wanted us to marry by water because the first time we got married was in the church. We wanted another spot that had a lake by it, and we look at it and said this is the place. I went in the building of this same location and tried to make it work. I couldn't see the vision, so I decided to do two locations. We planned to have some people coming out of town, and I didn't want them to get lost by having two locations. God really cares about your heart. A few months later, I went back to the place that we fell in love with, and they had tore down the old building and was building a new building. When this building was put up, it had the floor windows and was 2/3 cheaper than the first place. God just doesn't give you anything but the desires of your heart.

For this special day, I had to get my father blessing to walk me down the aisle. He eventually told me yes. It mattered to me because I'm a daddy's girl and I love my father with all my heart. The older I get, the more I realize that I act and think just like him. My father is the first man that I loved. When my mother passed, he continued raising me so I will always be in his debt. He has taught me some necessary lessons in life. For many years, when I was making bad choices in life, he protected me and caught me from my fall. He matters to me more than he is aware of. For example, I was a teen mother that was determined to finish high school. I had moved 2 ½ hours away from him, but the school needed his permission for everything. My father came to the school like he was down the street and had no job. He clearly was 2 ½ hours and had a full-time job because he believes in working hard. He might have fussed, but he came. You may not have a father like me, but God is willing to be your father. He will come when you need him. He is available to everybody and willing to guide you to wholeness and healing. You don't have to be perfect, but you do have to be willing to believe that he is real and ready to accept you with your broken pieces. Life is short, and I want you to live your best life. People are leaving here left and right, so we got to take advantage of every moment and be willing to surrender to God's Will.

When has God tried to be a father in your life?

_____

_____

_____

_____

_____

_____

_____

_____

_____

_____

Why have you rejected him?

_____

_____

_____

_____

_____

_____

_____

_____

_____

_____

_____

What thought in your head got to die so you can receive him?

_____

_____

_____

_____

_____

_____

_____

_____

_____

_____

My dress was important because, after my first wedding, my husband talked about how he thought I would have worn a wedding dress. I believe it mattered to him. One day, God asked me how a king can receive his queen if he has never seen her as one. I was determined to present myself as his queen. I had my dress designed with butterflies and diamonds. I am known for butterflies and speaking about the process of them. On my bouquet, I had my biological mother's picture on it and wore glittered tennis shoes. We went all out, and I made sure it was everything that I desired. It was worth every ounce of warfare I went through! I felt like a Cinderella! When I started dancing with my father, I needed him to know that I chose that song for him!! I started lip-singing it, so he would understand I appreciated his sacrifice. He just started crying!! This day was perfect, but it had many glitches. Our wedding planner had created a breathtaking atmosphere that set the tone of a miracle for people to witness what God had already done. These moments I will tell my children's children! God is faithful, and he loves me! I pray this encourages you to dream big again and believe that God can blow your mind.

Now, this honeymoon was the icing on the cake. We went to Savannah, Ga, and stayed at a hotel that was by the river. I had always wanted to go there and ready to go back. Once we parked the car, we walked everywhere and enjoyed each other's company. God has a way of loving you to peace and showing it is more to life than the one you are living. I am not sharing my story to brag but to let you know that God can do it for you too. I want to challenge the thoughts that the devil has told you and unlock hope and dreams.

What dreams have you let go of?

_____

_____

_____

_____

_____

_____

_____

_____

_____

_____

_____

_____

What is the devil trying to steal from your story?

_____

_____

_____

_____

_____

_____

_____

_____

_____

_____

_____

What is God stirring in your heart?

_____

_____

_____

_____

_____

_____

_____

_____

_____

_____

Why did you stop dreaming and believing that you didn't think mattered to God?

_____

_____

_____

_____

_____

_____

_____

_____

_____

_____

_____

_____

_____

_____

What have you thought about while reading this session?

_____

_____

_____

_____

_____

_____

_____

_____

_____

_____

_____

The Wait!

Have you ever made a cake? Whether the cake was from scratch or box, you had to put ingredients into it to complete it. Eggs, water, oil, flour, and sugar make the cake batter. Nobody puts the cake box or ingredients into the oven. You must mix things together, put it in a pan, pre-heat the oven, and set a timer. It is a whole process; it just doesn't happen. That is not including icing or making it pretty. I have never seen icing on a half-done cake. Think about it. Why do we try to dress up ourselves, and we have not yet gone through the process to be made whole? We are great about trying to fix the outer man and not working on the inner person. We must allow God space to help guide us through our pain and unhealed spots. We must give him permission to have his way in our life. It takes time and be open to wanting to be whole. Just like the cake, you cannot do it by yourself, you need developing into your purpose. Therefore, God gives us leaders and Pastor to guide us to a better place. Nobody is perfect, and we need somebody to make us better. On a side note, this is not your friend. How is a friend going direct you into a place they don't have any experience with? How are they going to pull out of you what they need pulled out of themselves? Our friends and family can be too familiar with us to help find new levels. They can encourage us but not lead us to purpose. You can't trust everybody so ask God to guide you to the person that will develop what

God put in you. You don't choose this person. In fact, when I asked God this question, I didn't even know my Pastor. I just knew it was more. You don't have to know everything, but your start is asking God for direction and listening to his direction. He didn't give that feeling for you to bury it but to give it back to him.

You must trust your leader in this season because the devil will try to use your flesh to move you out of position. If you move too quickly, it will be wasted time, and you won't manifest what the process was designed to produce. It will cause a lack or shortage of it. I have witnessed relationships destroyed because the student thought their time was up and God was just getting started. It is like preparing a great meal for your family for the holidays. You have prepared the atmosphere with a perfect setting that makes them feel the loved. You can smell and see the lights from candles on the table. Music plays in the background, and smiles are on your family and friends' faces. Everybody has gathered with their plate, silverware, and cup at the dining table. They are talking and laughing with each other. Here come the food, and it looks mouth-watering delicious. You can taste it in your mouth and can't wait to fix your plate. Can you see it? The dressing is golden brown and looks great. You can taste the greens with hot sauce. You make a big speech and prayer. You start cutting the chicken, it starts bleeding blood, and everything is messed up.

Nobody wants to eat anymore, and it doesn't matter about the decorations or how they felt. The chicken wasn't done and had been taken out too early, so it messes up everything. Your worst nightmare has manifested before your eyes. The same thing happens with our purpose. We have worked on the outer part and image. We have studied enough to sound and move a few heads. We have worked on our credit to the point that we can get a few things and a little money. If a real crisis come, we will crash. We have learned the presentation of the message, not the purpose behind it. We have the audacity to tell God that we are ready, and he just shakes his head because he sees the doors and opportunities that you are messing up. We must learn how to fully take God at his word.

We must trust the process and give ourselves time because we are worth the time. Our leader does have a flesh side, but we must understand that God gave them a spiritual side that they will obey his spirit no matter what. I have seen God use people that really didn't want to do it because what they knew about me. God has taught me so much in the waiting process that he is strong and faithful. He has taught me how to tame this flesh side that means me no good. I used to think I was ready, but I wasn't. I would have made a bigger mess of my life and others. I want to learn until the day I die. If you allow God, he will protect and keep you from yourself. Ask God what he is trying to show or teach you. We need to be more open to the things that God is revealing to us.

You must always use wisdom. You are no good for nobody if you have the knowledge and no wisdom. I went through a period in which I did a lot of interviews all over the United States and was on many people's live streamings on social media. I could have got the big head, but I stayed humbled. I remember a young lady asked me to speak with a group of ladies because I knew a few of them, I was willing to be of service. I asked God what he wanted me to say and started preparing. When I got on, I did like God asked me. The women was really moved to the point they wanted to sow into me. Then, a woman out of nowhere wanted to speak over my life. She told me that I should be in Evangelist school and that I needed to get under a leader that was going to support my ministry. She had called me after the call and everything. By the time the call ended, I was in my feeling and was ready to leave the church. I had to stop and take a step back to look at the whole picture. I began to ask God about the conversation and where I was at in life. Timing is everything! God began to tell me that he has destined me there, and He will show you, your time, and hour. He told me to trust the God in my leader, and I was on schedule. People from the outside will throw you off with their theory and plot if you allow them room in your ear. Don't let them. The devil knows your desire and will dress them up to make you fail. If you are growing in a place and developing your gifts, then be aware. You are a threat to satan, and he don't like it. See God called me to Destiny, and I knew that he had a plan for my life there.

Do you know God's plan for your life?

_____

_____

_____

_____

_____

_____

_____

When is the last time y'all talked about it?

_____

_____

_____

_____

_____

_____

Who do you trust to lead you? Why do you think you don't need to be led?

_____

_____

_____

_____

_____

_____

_____

_____

What do you think you are missing out of a leader?

_____

_____

_____

_____

_____

_____

_____

Why do you have trust problems?

_____

_____

_____

_____

_____

_____

_____

_____

_____

_____

_____

_____

_____

_____

_____

_____

_____

_____

_____

_____

Lion vs. Lamb

You have two sides of you that are working together to balance you out. On one side of you is a lamb, and on the other, you have a lion. A Lamb is soft and gentle. The side that is submitted and be silent so you can hear your leader speak. This Lamb side is great for prayer and getting an understanding. The side of the Lamb helps you fight the angry side of you not to destroy your relationships. Be a lamb when it is time for you to listen and receive correction. The Lion is the strong and bold side. When you want the enemy to know when you aren't playing games, then the lion roars. Have you ever felt something rise within you? It comes out of your spirit. This usually occurs when victory is near. This is what you use to get the enemy off your back. When a lion roars, you can hear them three to four miles. When it is time for you to fight, let the lion come out of you.

You need both sides. The Lamb doesn't win the battle; the Lion does. The devil will slay a lamb but doesn't know what to do with a Lion. The Lamb listens but the Lion answers and fights. The Lion side demands structure and order. People don't know how to handle this side of you because it challenges them to do better. If you don't put your foot down in the natural, the devil will take advance of you in the spirit. It is a part of your life that in natural realm you must be able say enough is enough. This is when you learn the power of No. Satan wants to use the weak side of you when you need to be strong. The Lion side must kick in and take some territory in some seasons. You must use your discernment to know when to be what. You don't have time to cry because we are too close to victory. You could lose this whole fight because you are trying to cry or complain at the wrong time. You are about to cross the line and don't see it because the lamb side overrides the lion side.

Lambs need to be led. When it is time to get the victory, the Lion rises. At the end of a battle, we get tired, so Don't allow your body to determine how loud you roar. Let your body catch up with your spirit. Walk into your boldness and strength and be who God allows you to be. Don't get them mixed up. You can't be a lion when you need to be led and a lamb when you need to fight. You must know the moment and what God called you to be. You must make sure things are in proper order. It is a part of you that must answer a thing and put it in check.

When I think about trying to decide whether to be a lamb or a lion, I think about parenting. Sometimes your children need you to be a lamb. They need you to teach them, read them stories, and watch movies. Most of the time, we educate them in and out of lamb mode because they need compassion and guidance in life. Then there are other times you must bring the lion out when they want to fight against where you are trying to lead them. When they bump

up against you and want their way, your lion side
must come out.

When has God revealed that you have a lion in you?

_____

_____

_____

_____

_____

_____

_____

_____

_____

_____

When has he shown you that you were a lamb?

_____

_____

_____

_____

_____

_____

_____

_____

_____

**When have you been a lamb and was supposed to
be a lion?**

_____

_____

_____

_____

_____

_____

_____

_____

_____

_____

_____

_____

When have you been a lion and was supposed to be a lamb?

_____

_____

_____

_____

_____

_____

_____

_____

How can you use this information and make your future better?

_____

_____

_____

_____

_____

_____

_____

_____

The Power of Connection

God has always connected me with people that see my greatness and help me express it. Believe it or not, I wasn't never aggressive; I just took what life gave me. I could be bleeding and not move. I would run toward it when you could show how it would benefit somebody else. It is power in who you are connected to, God uses connections for your good, and the devil uses them for your bad. If God is showing that your time is up in a place, and you won't move because you are comfortable with those around you, it is disobedience. I was at a job for many years, and I knew my time was up. I was over everything and ready for change. One way you can be aware of it is time to leave is by asking yourself questions. Are you too comfortable? Are you learning, and is it benefiting you by being there?

I had a conversation with my cousin through my husband. I began sharing with him about how frustrated I was and ready to leave. He asked me why I won't leave. I told him that I was waiting on my husband, and he said, "maybe he is waiting on you." I thought for a minute. Maybe he was waiting on me because I knew that he was tired too. So, I started planning my move. Listen, once my husband realized that I was leaving this company, he started making his moves. In fact, he started his new job before I did. There were so many opportunities for growth and development in my next job.

I remember being out of work for a year because of my health and other things that were happening in my life. I was ready to go back to work and move forward in my business, so I needed funds to help with the process. God used a connection of a best friend/sister, Nafeesah. When I finally decided to take her up on her opportunity, I was in awe of God's plan. This was one of the highest-paying jobs that I had in the corporate world, and the workload was lighter. I worked, but it was more mental than physical work, so it was a different lane. We had a lot of freedom and were not limited in movement, like bathroom and breaks. It was just different for me. It is interesting that people will pay us more for our minds than physical labor. We feel more value when we do physical work. I really don't understand why. Maybe it is because we are trained that way. I have always felt it was something about physically working hard.

I stayed with my sister for about three years; I watched her work so hard it made me mad. One thing I can say is my sister didn't mind climbing the ladder. She made a bad situation be amazing. I moved down there with her when I found out I was expecting. A few months later, she revealed that she was expecting her second child. I said reveal because she was aware of it. Thinking about it brings tears to my eyes because she loves me beyond herself. She taught me how to survive and pull the best out of life. Our babies are eleven days apart and of opposite sexes. We were about a month away from our expected dates and didn't have any clothes for our kids. She said we could get five onesies a piece. Are you getting boy or girl clothes? I wanted to have a boy, so I picked out boy clothes. She looked at our belly and said I'm the opposite of you, so I'll get girl clothes. I had the girl, and she had the boy. Don't overlook blood connections because I wouldn't have survived without her. I remember we used to push the kids in strollers to the grocery store, and on the way back, we used them as a cart. I needed her, and she stepped up to be there for me. She loves my kids like they are her, and I love her kids like they are mine.

Who has God placed in your life that you have overlooked?

_____

_____

_____

_____

_____

_____

_____

_____

How have they helped you be better?

_____

_____

_____

_____

_____

_____

_____

_____

_____

What doors have you walked through because of your connection?

_____

_____

_____

_____

_____

_____

_____

Who are you grateful for?

_____

_____

_____

_____

_____

_____

_____

_____

_____

_____

Who have you helped walk in doors?

_____

_____

_____

_____

_____

_____

_____

_____

_____

_____

_____

_____

_____

Who can you help today walk into a new place?

_____

_____

_____

_____

_____

_____

_____

_____

_____

_____

_____

Believe Again

If God has called you, there will be attacks. They come to distract and change your mind. I have come to put life in the things that you were about to walk away from because it is not over, but it is just a beginning. I know you thought God forgot, but he was just waiting for you to trust him.

In our first house, I desired two Christmas trees. Not because I was being extra, but I just kept seeing two. I would tell my husband, son, and friends that I was going to have two. I had decided that I wanted one to match my furniture in the living room. I wanted it to be traditional in the family room, with red, green, and gold. One day I got a text asking me if I wanted a Christmas tree and some ornaments. I got so excited when he brought the tree because it was an answered prayer. God is amazing and will give you the desires of your heart. Even down to the ornaments, they were the color that I needed them to be. We must understand that we matter to God; He doesn't want us to settle because He has the best for us. I would not leave it in the box because I wanted to show God that I was grateful for him answering my prayers. To really understand this chapter, you must break the belief system that you don't matter. I had to believe beyond my money and situation. God just wants you to believe, and it is his job to manifest the way he desires. If you look for him through the right door, he will come through the left one. God doesn't want us to get comfortable or limit how he comes through for us. I believe that he allowed Lazarus to die to show us that he could do the impossible. When you take the chains off of your miracle, it can manifest into your life.

God really started to deal with me about this because he wants to blow my mind. I was talking to one of my friends at work about needing some lemons because my throat was hurting. I knew tea and lemon would help me better. I didn't have time to be sick or not feel my best because I had goals and dreams to manifest. We went along with our day and continued to work. She dropped me off at the house, and I went through the door and walked through my family room and then the kitchen. I walk in the Foyer and out the door to check the mail. It was a brown plastic bag on my porch. Guess what was in the bag? LEMONS! They were lemons that came from somebody's tree, not the story. Stop limiting God and believe God can use anybody and do anything. I take off the limits of God and just enjoy him loving on me.

You must learn to trust your instinct because it will guide you to the door that God promised. Everything is not going to come the same way, and you must be open to new ways. You can't get comfortable with God. Have you ever been in a relationship and noticed things have changed? He used to take you out on the town, then it stopped. Or she used to cook soul food, and now she has been bringing in take-out. Now, it is a season in life when you must adjust to what is going on, but I'm talking about no major event happening. You must remind people of your value when they get comfortable with you. God doesn't allow us to get comfortable with him. He is always changing up. He never changes. The way that he comes through you is always changing. We must use our instincts to move with God. We can miss out on a whole blessing by second-guessing what is calling us to desire more. I was totally in the way of what God had purposed me to be. I wanted to be simple and in the background. Does this sound familiar to you? It is our comfort zone and safe place. I get it. Nothing manifests in your comfort zone.

There comes a time in your life when you must value yourself. I have known for many years that I was called to entrepreneurship. When I got a glimpse of what I desired and wanted in life, I realized that 9 to 5 wasn't going to pay for it. It was over in my mind. I do believe that God has used the jobs that I have been on to educate me on what to do and what not to do. Throughout the years, I have learned how to value myself and not put all my value in my job. Because I knew that I was just passing through and climbing the ladder, we would give a job everything, and then we get mad at the job. In fact, some of the things that you are mad about, you volunteered and did it because you felt obligated to do it. Nobody asked you; you just moved. Don't get mad at yourself just change your movement. Know who you are and value it. Break the chains off your mind and the mental thoughts you put in your mind. God has more for you, and his goal is not for you to be a slave to your boss. You must have boundaries and limits in everything. You must balance your life and value what God placed on your life. Free yourself from the chains, and don't wait on somebody to do it for you. Stir up your own gift and make a move. God will meet you once you open the door for him to come in. It starts with you and your belief system. I challenge you to allow your inner beauty to shine for your purpose. You have let everybody go before you, and now it is your time to shine. The world will not end; somebody will stay stuck if you don't move into your purpose. If you don't do it for yourself, do it for them.

How does your thinking limit you from thinking bigger?

_____

_____

_____

_____

_____

_____

_____

_____

Why do you think small?

_____

_____

_____

_____

_____

_____

_____

_____

Where did this come from?

_____

_____

_____

_____

_____

_____

_____

_____

Who in your life made you feel that you didn't matter?

_____

_____

_____

_____

_____

_____

_____

What has manifested in your comfort zone besides troubles and problems?

_____

_____

_____

_____

_____

_____

_____

What boundaries do you need to set?

_____

_____

_____

_____

_____

_____

_____

_____

What could you accomplish if you set them in place?

_____

_____

_____

_____

_____

_____

_____

_____

A Set Place

My prayer is that you find your set place that God has chosen for you to develop in and pull the greatest out of you. You must believe that God cares enough for you to be taught so you can teach others. You must submit to the process, and trusting God is necessary. You never choose your set place, but it chooses you. I never knew that I was a prophet or was worthy of any of God's calling on my life. My spiritual father, Dr. Jevon Goode, has been a blessing to my life and calling. He has opened and expanded my thoughts of God in ways that I never knew were possible. Destiny Church in Dothan was my set place. I learn how to get free of myself and see things as God sees them. People never understood our relationship, but I didn't care. He didn't choose me either, but after a while, God talked to both of us. God's plan was better for my life because he has walked me into doors, experiences, and moments that I never thought I would be. Connections matter for growth and develop you for purpose. You are not going to agree on everything. In fact, I want real people in my life, not yes, ma'am people. They agree with you no matter what you say, but in their minds, they don't. I would come to church broken, and Pastor J would have a word that would shift my thinking or heal a wound. It matters to me, and this is where God started to open my eyes to our relationship. Things take time, and you can't rush this process. Let God talk to him and wait for guidance.

You never want somebody to guide you unwillingly. You want their heart right and in a position, for God to use you.

You must have wisdom about when to start something and when to pass the torch to the next person in line. I pour out daily to the people around me because I want to leave this world empty. I remember watching a movie called "Biker Boyz." The movie's ending is the best part because the leader shows control and strength and is called Smoke. He has raced the younger biker for his crown (position), which is called Kid. It is a lot of trenching between them, like Smoke just found out that he is Kid's father. It is a great movie that has nuggets in it. As they begin to race, Smoke gets focused on the race and gets his mind together. As they are riding down the dirt road, his mind starts going back to other events and moments that he previously had about this young man with other people. Toward the end, something is exchanged between the two men because Kid starts getting focused. The race was very close. Smoke backed off at the end and allowed Kid to win at the last second. As a parent, I can understand this because winning the position causes you to grow up. We want victory but don't always see the weight of the position. After we have the position, we see the weight and the responsibility of it clearer. Some lessons you don't learn until you get in the position. As a leader, we must know when to pass the torch and pull back so our next can win. They have this moment after the race where Kid tells Smoke that he can keep his hamlet. For most of the movie, people have been trying to get this helmet, and he gives it back. That is a moment of growth. He didn't boast about it, but he opened his heart. We can win more battles if we open our hearts instead of boasting.

When is the last place that you felt God's presence?

_____

_____

_____

_____

_____

_____

_____

What is the place that you don't want to go back to and why?

_____

_____

_____

_____

_____

_____

_____

_____

_____

What did God say about it? Did the assignment get fulfilled?

_____

_____

_____

_____

_____

_____

_____

_____

_____

_____

_____

_____

What are you waiting on?

_____

_____

_____

_____

_____

_____

_____

_____

_____

What will happen if you are obedient to God's voice?

_____

_____

_____

_____

_____

_____

_____

_____

A Leader's Legacy

You have made it to the last chapter, and my prayer is that your perspective has shifted toward God's purpose for your life. And this book will be a tool to help develop you into the person God has called you to be.

This book would not be complete without the impartation of my pastor/spiritual father, Dr. Jevon Goode. He is a very busy man and always has something to do, so it was an honor for me to interview him and for him to share his wisdom with me. I'm asking the questions, and he is answering the questions. I pray this blesses you as much as it blessed me because we don't always get to hear or read the rawness and realness of our leader.

This is how our conversation went...

What is your view on spiritual sons and daughters? Why do you think they're necessary?

Well, sons & daughters are different from just regular congregants because sons and daughters have gifts that are going to keep the legacy of ministry going, so you know the sons of the prophets. These were those connected close to the prophet, but they had prophetic gifts that were being developed. So when it comes down to sons and daughters, these are the people whose gifts will keep not only that ministry running, but they are also gifts that are going to step out of that ministry and do other things outside of that ministry. So sons and daughters have a twofold purpose. They keep the ministry that they're part of moving, but they also tend to move in and out of that ministry, whether it's, you know they're traveling, whether they're pastoring, whether they're leading whatever the case may be, but they still stay connected to that spiritual father/mother. - Dr. Jevon Goode

What are some things that you have learned from our relationship?

I think the biggest thing has been loyalty, which has been a very good thing, and your ability to listen. You're teachable. There are sons and daughters for seasons, and the seasons don't always have reasons connected to them. Sometimes people will be sons and daughters because of that spiritual father's popularity. So they look at what they can gain from it. Some of them are not there for relationships. They're there for whatever doors will open for them because they are connected to this specific person. -Dr. Jevon Goode

With us, you're not connected to me because of my name or my doors or any of those things. You connected to me because of the value that you see in me imparting to your life and making you better not just from ministry but just in general, as a woman, as a mother, as a daughter, as a prisoner, as a minister, all those things. So the loyalty. You know the ability to be teachable. The ability to not be so easily offended and one of the great things that I've seen is that there's no guile. You are just who you are. So you don't put on the airs, you know what I'm saying, you're just who you are. I think, also, the level of respect that you have. Not just for me but the level of respect that you have for the relationship. Right now, you know I got a million things going on. You know what I'm saying, But you know how to be patient enough with my schedule. You know so that it will fit into what's going on with you, where some people will automatically, because of the lack of respect, feel rejected if they don't get that particular time. And you don't; you don't do. -Dr. Jevon Goode

I think I kind of learned that from under your ministry because you have taught me an extended amount of patience. I've always been patient, but you taught me how to have extra patience. It's like when you look at a box instead of just looking at two sides. Turn the box to see the other side. You can see the other sides and focus on the whole picture. You must learn patience is the key.

And if there was another word or an extra word for patience, the other side of patience is understanding. So once you turn that box, you're able to kind of see from the other person's point of view, which gives you that level of understanding too. -Dr. Jevon Goode

Can Spiritual Sons & daughters be seasonal, or are they long-term? Like Marcus Tankard, he has been your spiritual son for a long time. How do you know the difference?

When it comes down to members, members have the possibility of being short-term. When it comes down to sons and daughters, that's a covenant. Those relationships really should not be seasonal. They really shouldn't be. If you are mentoring someone, like say, someone wants you to mentor them. You can mentor them to a specific degree or specific place, and that could be seasonal. But once people start talking about being sons and daughters, that really should be for a lifetime. Now again, because of the agendas of some people, you know, they seek out who they want to call, you know, pop or right, spiritual father, spiritual mother, whatever the case might be. But when it's really God, it's never a seasonal thing; it is a journey. -Dr. Jevon Goode

Elijah and Elisha when Elijah met Elisha. There was something about Elijah that Elisha needed. And even after Elijah left, Elisha kept Elijah's name going. The first miracle that he performed, he said. The God of Elijah. He kept his name going, so that's the reason I say with spiritual sons and daughters. They should keep the name of them, of the Spiritual father/mother moving. Whether he's still on the earth or spiritual mother still on earth or even if they've gone home to

The Lord, they should still be keeping that name moving. If I say seasonal, Really, to be honest with you, those relationships should be lifetime warranties. Usually, if they're seasonal, it's because there is some level of agenda that is connected to it. -Dr. Jevon Goode

You have said several times that you can't pick your spiritual children, or you don't pick your spiritual father or mother. And I believe that because I believe that you were my spiritual father before I even knew who you were. I remember hearing you on the radio, and something in me would jump and get excited. How do you know on your end? Is it a feeling? Is it something that you experience or something God told you? How do you know who is your spiritual sons and daughters? One thing I do know about you is that you're very intentional, and you don't just claim people just to own or cover them; you got too much to do to do that, so how do you know that somebody is your spiritual son or daughter?

At one point, when it was all about Ego for me, I would claim people as spiritual sons and daughters out of flattery. So if they flattered me enough and they said, you know, you're my spiritual father, blah blah blah, I would take him in. Now I realize that being a father is more about connection. It's a God connection, so it's something that, like you said before, you ever came to know me. You would hear me on the radio and something, the things that I would say, my voice inspired your voice. My life inspired your life, so for me now is, I look to see if there's something in me in them already. If I can't see that, then we're not supposed to be connected. But if I can sense that there's something in me, that's in them. Also, something in them that no one can bring out of them but me, and I can feel that God's connection, then they're a spiritual son or daughter. -Dr. Jevon Goode

But I've also realized that no man or woman needs to have just spiritual sons and daughters everywhere because then it's no longer special. So there's a limit for me, You know. Those who I need to father and who I'm just to lead, and who I'm just to preach. My spiritual children are limited. It's very few, and that helps me because I know who I've been partnered to, and I can keep up with them in the spirit. Instead of saying I'm a spiritual father of 50, some odd sons and daughters. And you can't keep up with them like that. -Dr. Jevon Goode

That goes back to what you said about the egos. Just looking at various of your spiritual children, you know you have some that are

famous, some that are not known yet. You have some that sing, some musicians, some that are authors. Is it anything that you can see amongst all of us, that our ways we connect?

Yeah, for sure I do, and it's the aspect of being able to get everyone to meet each other so that they get a chance to see what they can do to help each other in those, you know, those particular areas. I think that everyone that our Father has something for each other, and I see those areas, so I'm not writing books, but you are. You know. I'm saying I'm not leading prayer, but Marcus does, you know? So yeah, there, there's so many different ones that whatever there sphere of influence is, it does, and will literally blend over into the other sons and daughters. -Dr. Jevon Goode

Do you see any difference in leading women and men? because I have heard you teach about women can be very emotional, and men can be prideful or something like that, but is it anything that, whether it's good or bad in the difference leading sons or daughters?

Sometimes, it's no different. No different because sometimes you know sons can be emotional, and the women can be intentional, and sometimes the women can be prideful, and the sons can have a level of humility. The gender doesn't matter. -Dr. Jevon Goode

How do you or what experience have you learned to set boundaries with your spiritual children? Like how do you set down boundaries?

But thus far, all my spiritual kids are respectful, so there's been no reason to say, hey, Don't call me, currently. They don't text me currently or nothing like that. Everybody respects my time. They respect my schedule, they respect who I am, and so I really haven't had to set any boundaries. I'm involved as much as my children allow me to be involved in their world. And the stuff that I'm not involved in, I just pray about, and the things that you know I feel led to kind of talk about it talk about. For me, it's not a one-way street. You know, like with some spiritual fathers and spiritual mothers, it's, you know, that child, a spiritual child always having to call them or approach them, and for me, I'll take the time to stop and say, hey, how's everything going? What's going on? So boundaries have never been an issue for me as it relates to spiritual children. -Dr. Jevon Goode

They say that you can learn from anybody. Is there anything that you could say that you have learned from your spiritual children?

Yeah, I've learned a lot. I've learned aspects of resilience. I've learned aspects of especially with you.

You have a tenacious drive. You know you're going to get to whatever it is that God's put in your heart, you're not backing off it. I love that, and I learned from that, and that's a push for me. You know, I'm saying I can see that part of me in you, but at the same time you inspire that part in me. If this is what God says, I'm going for it. Each spiritual child teaches me something specific. -Dr. Jevon Goode

If you could say anything to your spiritual kids, or if you could say anything you feel led to say. What would it be?

To be honest with you, everything for me revolves around walking by faith. I know that's a very simple thing, but it is the biggest thing because you always have people say, you know keep God first, do this, do that, whatever. My biggest thing is to each spiritual child is to always believe God for all things, that's it. You know, always believe God for all things. My Pastor, the late David Pizzimenti, wrote in one of my Bibles under Mark 11:22 through 23, which was, I learned faith from him. And he put in one of my Bibles, and I have that Bible in my office. He wrote "this will work for you," and that meant a lot because I watched him. I came into his life after the fact, but he built a $1.4 million building. He did all these things, all these things he did by Faith, and so him being able to say that to me was enough for me to hold on to, and so I say it to spiritual kids. You know, whatever you do, **BELIEVE GOD FOR ALL THINGS**, yeah. -Dr. Jevon Goode

Closing Remarks

We get so excited about getting to the end of something, title, or position. What we should realize is that at the end is a new start. **Why are we excited for the next? Do we realize that the end is death?** We must be careful because some positions carry weight, and they will destroy us. God will manifest it when you are designed or called to a plait. We must stay out of the way and allow him to be God.

Did you know that Edward VIII abdicated his title as king because he wanted to marry an adulteress woman. Because he did this, his brother became King, and Queen Elizabeth was in line for the queen. When God ordains something, it will happen, so stop worrying about something that you have no control over.

You must be aware of the time that you are in because somebody could be preparing you for your next, and you are not aware. They could be intentionally sent to you in room or on a trip to prepare you for your next. You must be aware of these people in your life so you can take advantage of the moment. Get all the wisdom that the moment gives you to receive. You must be aware of the people that are meant to pour into your life. These people can be seasonal in your life, so do not get upset when their season is up. For example, I work a job and found favor with my director for a season. As I look back, it was really a God connection and move. The things that she taught me, I will use them until I die. I'm so grateful for her and who she was to my life in that season. Make sure you honor and respect the place and people that God allows you to come across. You must realize that you are enough and open your superpower. Everybody has a superpower. You are probably using it and not even aware of it. It is that thing we love to do and would do it for free. Through the years, I learned that I have several, most of them, have to do with my mouth. I realize when I tell people what God said, it gives them confirmation and helps them on their journey. Your superpower is not for you. God uses it so you will find favor with man. Believe in who God has called you to be. You matter, and we need you in these streets. I can't wait to hear the stories and testimony from this book because I have had some attacks and frustration moments, but it is well, and you are worth it. Your story matters, and I believe in you! You can send your review to mrsque2020@gmail.com or on Amazon.

We thank you for your time in telling us how this book has touched your life. For more books and information on Que'Nona Guilford go to www.mrsque.com. Thank you for supporting Mrs. Que's movement. Please continue to pray for it and what God wants to do through it.

Word From The Author

My name is Que'Nona Guilford. As far as I can remember, God has always been with me. I have tried to walk away from Him several times, but He has always embraced me with open arms. I don't remember when I got saved, but I clearly remember when my walk got serious. I remember hearing and learning "Jesus Loves me" as a little girl. It was this church that was down the street from my house where I had fallen in love with God, and I wanted to know more. The people were so nice and never treated me any different because of my skin. I remember one day as my sister, and I was walking out the door, and my younger brother had burned himself with grease trying to get some fries. After we saw that he was going to be ok. We started heading for the door, and my father stopped us and asked where we were going. We looked back at him and said to church. He looked at us, crazy and confused. I remember saying something like, I'll pray for him at church. It was like I could hear the church calling my soul, and I was ready to answer.

As I look back on my life, God has always been there and showing up for me. My life has grace all over it. The only way that I got here was through God. I don't look like what I've been through. I have no signs of rape, rejection, abandonment, teen mother, single mother, and insecure woman because God has a way of healing before he reveals you. God has allowed me to overcome it and learn how to help people to come out of this by challenging their perceptive. Your perception is the door to your purpose. If you think you can, you will. If you think that you can't, you won't. When I decided that I would have everything that God desired for my life. My life changed for the better. It is not perfect, but it is purpose-filled. I moved out of God's way and allowed him to move into my life. He has shown me that all he wanted me to do.

ABOUT THE AUTHOR

Que'Nona Guilford is a God-fearing, activating faith, spirit-driven, and a rising powerhouse in the kingdom of God. She takes great pleasure in seeking after God's heart and desires to discover more of His will for her life. She is committed wife to her husband and loving mother of four children (Billie, Aaliyah, Noah and Joshua).

Que'Nona is a domestic violence survivor, and with that being a major aspect in her life, she desires to bring awareness to the issue in her community. A Change In Me Domestic Violence Awareness Event was birthed out of her past experiences.

Que'Nona is an author of four other books called The Moments When God Touched, Gleaning To Legacy: The Next Generation, Gleaning To Legacy: The Next Level, Leaping Into Purpose and S.O.S. 30 day Devotional Speaking Over Storms. They are all available on Amazon and you can get more information on her website at www.mrsque.com. She also loves being a Mary Kay consultant.

Que'Nona received the Inaugural Girlfriend Award in November of 2018 and Outstanding Community Service Award from Zeta Phi Beta Sorority in March of 2019.

Made in the USA
Columbia, SC
01 April 2024

33444218R00067